Horse Racing Form Guide

Contents

My Personal Details

My Background

Horse Racing Form Guide For Handicap Races In The UK

Why People Struggle To Understand UK Horse Racing Form

What Are The Key Horse Form Variables For UK Handicap Races

A Detailed Example Of A UK Handicap Horse Race

Some Example UK Handicap Horse Races

Using The Horse Form Guide In UK Non Handicap Horse Races

Using The Horse Form Guide Additional Filters

Recommended Sites

My Other Books On Amazon

Available in eBook and paperback.

Most Profitable Horse Racing System Kindle Edition
https://www.amazon.co.uk/dp/B08QDNWV56

Horse Racing System Seeing The Light Kindle Edition
https://www.amazon.co.uk/dp/B08LL4PWQP

Groupform UK Horse Racing System Kindle Edition
https://www.amazon.co.uk/dp/B084M4FSWN

Best Horse Racing System Kindle Edition
https://www.amazon.co.uk/dp/B084V9S4Z7

Picking Winners No Problem: Horse Racing Betting System Kindle Edition
https://www.amazon.co.uk/dp/B08BJXMN3R

UK Horse Racing Handicap System: Took 2 Years To Computer Model Kindle Edition
https://www.amazon.co.uk/dp/B084VRDL8T

Betfair Place Market UK Horse Handicap System: Horse Racing Betting System Kindle Edition
https://www.amazon.co.uk/dp/B089FHPSM7

Horse Racing Betting Secret System: UK Horse Racing System To Change Your Betting Kindle Edition
https://www.amazon.co.uk/dp/B08CVSZW39

UK Professional Horse Racing Betting Edge Kindle Edition
https://www.amazon.co.uk/dp/B08JM3FV4M

Horse Racing Betting Dutching System Kindle Edition
https://www.amazon.co.uk/dp/B08BDN5VGK

The 6f 7f Furlong Hope Horse Lay System Simple To Use And Profitable Kindle Edition
https://www.amazon.co.uk/dp/B084RHCCSX

The Two Step Horse Racing System Kindle Edition
https://www.amazon.co.uk/dp/B084QHSKYH

UK Horse Racing Betting Systems Paperback – 7 Feb. 2020
https://www.amazon.co.uk/dp/B084DGQNKK

My Personal Details

Please check out my articles on my website if you have any questions please do not hesitate to contact me.

Website: https://chevanderwheil.com/

Email: vanderwheil6@gmail.com

My Background

Many people who have bought my books must know my background by now!

In a nutshell I am a passionate horse racing punter and Betfair trader who enjoys his work every day how lucky am I? I was a freelance I.T. consultant for 30 years specialising in relational databases on Unix platforms. I used this I.T. skill to model horse racing in the UK using many years of past results I had loaded into my bespoke database. I am not going to dwell on this.

Horse Racing Form Guide For Handicap Races In The UK

After many years of modelling handicap horse racing form I eventually discovered the key horse form variables that identify the best handicapped horses in a particular UK horse race. I must stress this was not an easy journey as I would model a number of UK handicap horse races noting down key horse form variable patterns that identified the best horses in the race only to be disappointed. I repeated this modelling 1000's of times over 10 years of horse form data. Eventually my patience and tenacity allowed me to identify the best horse form variables that can be applied to a UK handicap horse race. More importantly I was impressed how consistent these horse variables were over 100's of horse races in selecting the best horses.

In this horse racing form guide I will outline the most effective way to read horse form for UK handicap horse races effectively and consistently and quickly as we all lead busy lives.

Why People Struggle To Understand UK Horse Racing Form

In my earlier years of reading horse form in UK handicap horse races I struggled, I could not link the key horse form variables like weight, the official rating of the horse and race distance and many more. If you have a 12 runner horse race by the time I had analysed the form for the 6th horse in the race I had forgotten the other horses I had just analysed. When you add emotion into this such as focusing on a horse you are fond of regardless of its form you are distracted. Another common problem I had when reading horse form was everyday distractions such as the dog barking or somebody at the door. In the early days I used a manual process noting down horse form variables and constant back checking, it was a labour intensive process each horse race taking 20 to 30 minutes to analyse the horse form. Now there are on average four UK horse race meeting per day so there was a great deal of work to be done. Two of the major factors people struggle when reading horse form is concentration and fatigue. We now have computer software to crunch data more effectively and quickly and more importantly it is less prone to human error.

We should not be fooled and think that advancements in technology is our success route to reading horse form data it just allows us to do it more efficiently, remember the phrase 'GIGO' garbage in garbage out. So what do I mean by this? Well, even with a computer processing the data you need to know what horse form variables to look for when analysing a horse race effectively.

There are a number of excellent horse form guide computer applications out there but these applications tend to work using horse form filters like did the horse finish 2nd and has the horse won on the course and distance and many more. What you get when you apply these filters are not always the best horses for a particular handicap horse race. These filters do eliminate to some degree horses with bad form or unsuitable courses and distances but deeper horse form analysis is needed to identify the best horses of a race. I will cover this in detail in later chapters.

What Are The Key Horse Form Variables For UK Handicap Races

The horse racing form guide uses the excellent website racing post which is free and this is all you need. I also recommend using the Betfair betting exchange to obtain better prices.

https://www.racingpost.com

https://www.betfair.com/

Let's get started!

In this chapter I will delve deeper into key horse form variables that will make a difference to your horse form reading.

The CV Horse Form Variable

The first horse form variable we are interested in is the horse consistency value and we will refer to this variable as **CV**. So what is this variable CV? This variable is the sum value of the horse's last 3 finishing positions in it's last 3 races. So for example if **Horse A** finished 1st, 2nd, 1st in it's last three races then the CV value would be 1+2+1=4 so CV would be equal to 4. With this horse form variable we are interested in a CV value of no greater than the value 7. When we look at the last races for a horse we pick any type of race. If a horse fell or was pulled up we look at the next last race. The beauty of this horse form variable is that it will eliminate most of the horses in a race. This means we have less work to do when applying the next horse form variables.

The WV Horse Form Variable

Now we will take a look at our next horse form variable, this to me is the most important variable when reading horse form. This horse form variable is associated with the weight it carried in its last race and the weight the horse is running off in the UK handicap horse race you are analysing. We need to establish if the horse is carrying less or more weight by comparing the last race weight to the current race weight. We will call this horse form variable **WV**. We are only interested in horses where the weight difference is <=1. A typical example below,

Horse A last race weight 9-10 (9 stone 10 pounds)

Horse A current race (Todays Race) weight 9-3 (9 stone 3 pounds)

Convert the horse weight to pounds

129 Pounds (9-3) – 136 Pounds (9-10) = -7 pounds less.

So our weight horse form variable **WV** is -7 pounds.

This value of -7 pounds is less than or equal to our filter of less than equal to 1 pound. We are only interested in weight difference of less than or equal to 1.

At this stage we have covered two horse form variables **CV** and **WV** these will eliminate most horses in a UK handicap race.

The BV Horse Form Variable

The BV horse form variable is the difference between the horse's current race BHB rating (Official Rating OR) and it's second last race BHB rating.

BV= current race BHB rating- second last race BHB rating

The BV variable must have a value of >=0 and <=4

Example

Horse A 2nd last race BHB rating 67

Horse A current race BHB rating 68

BV=68-67=1

So horse A **BV** variable value is within range >=0 and <=4

Very few horses will be left after this step and we only have the final horse form variable to consider.

The LV Horse Form Variable

The LV horse form variable is the horse's last race finishing position and this must be in the range of 1st to 5th position if the horse had finished greater than 5th position you dismiss the horse. This is an easy horse form variable to analyse.

Form Horse Form Variables Summary

The four horse form variables we have discussed earlier are,

CV – Horse Consistency Value   (Acceptable range less than equal to 7).

WV – Horse Weight Value (Acceptable range less than equal to 1).

BV – Horse BHB Value (Acceptable range greater than equal to 0 and less than equal to 4).

LV – Horse Last Finishing Position (Acceptable range must have finished 1st 2nd 3rd 4th 5th in last race).

When reading horse form data by calculating the value for these four horse form variables above this will filter the best horses in a race. Now you might have 2 or 3 best horses in a race so extra horse form reading is needed for each of these horses. You can back all three horses if the odds permit this or you could dutch these horses it's up to you.

A Detailed Example Of A UK Handicap Horse Race

In this chapter I will show you a detailed example of a UK handicap horse race where I have applied these key four horse form variables.

2nd February 2021 Southwell 7.40 Palazzo 100/30 Won

Below are the horse form variables for the winner of the race Palazzo which each variable value qualified.

CV=7 WV=1 BV=1 LV=3

For a horse to qualify as a selection the four horse form variables must be within the valid range.

See race result screenshot below.

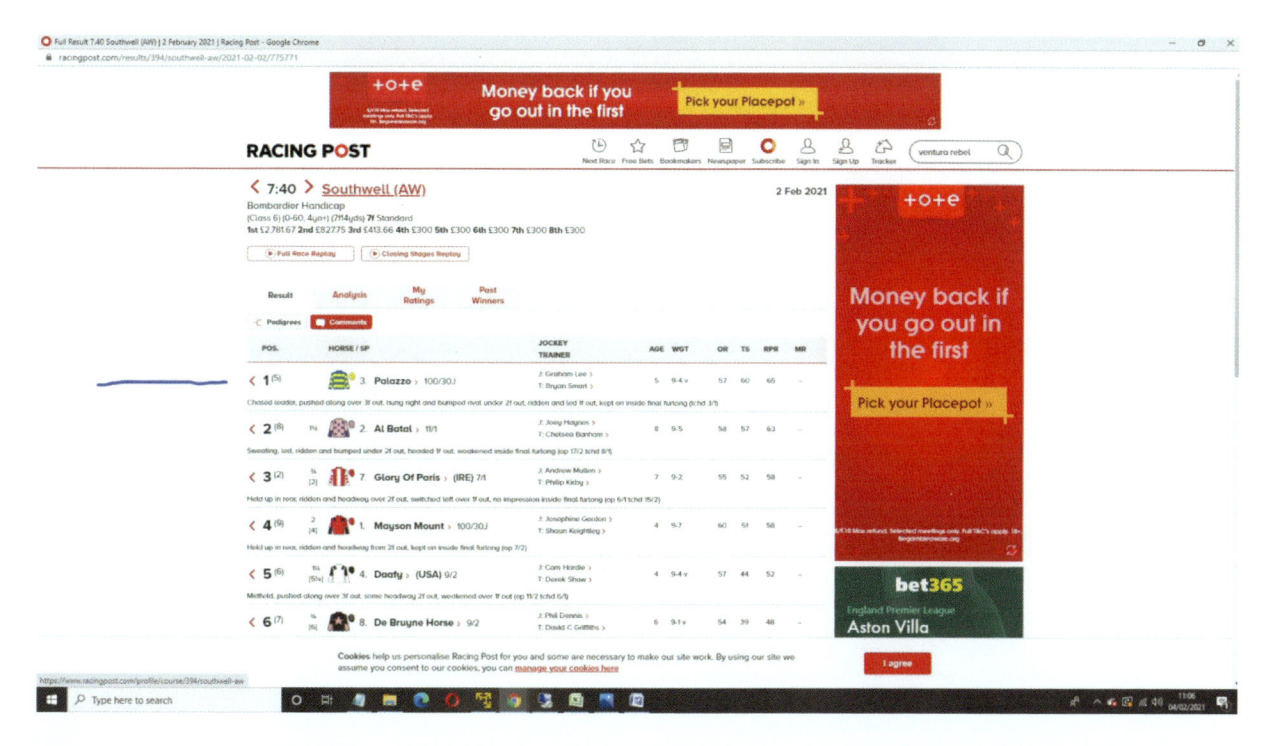

Please look at screenshots below to see how the four horse form variables were derived for the horse Palazzo. We would have had to apply the process to all the horses in that race. This process is relatively straight forward.

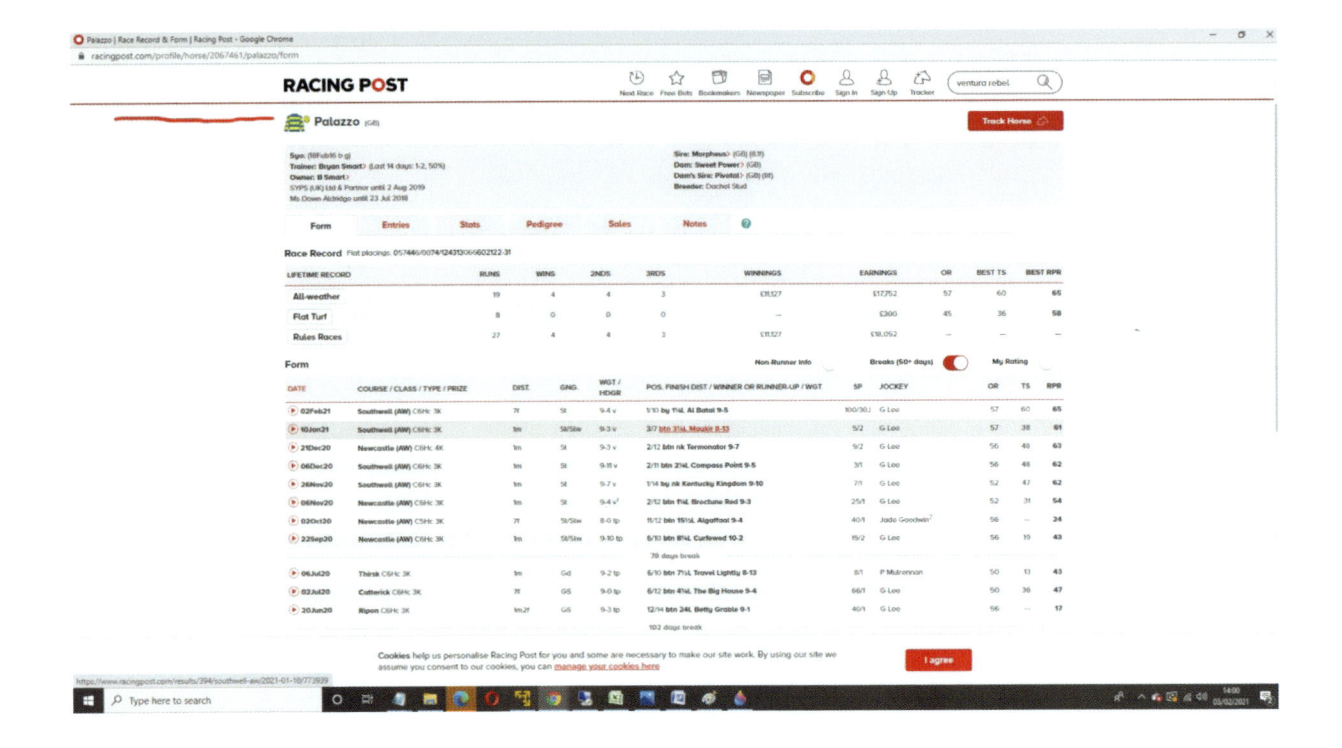

Using the screenshot below I have highlighted in different colours the key areas to take note of when calculating the four horse form variables.

The horse Palazzo won the race on the 2nd February 2021 highlighted in blue below. We calculate the CV variable by adding the last 3 races position which are 3rd 2nd 2nd which is CV=3+2+2 which is 7 and passes this filter.

We now calculate the WV which is today's race weight 9-4 minus last race weight 9-3 underlined in green which is +1 pound extra weight so our WV variable value is 1 so passes this filter.

We now calculate the BV variable we look at the horse's second last race which was 21st December 2021 with BHB OR – official rating of 56 underlined in red. The horses current OR is 57 underlined in orange. So the BV variable value is 57-56=1 so passes this filter.

On to our last horse form variable LV this is the horse's last race position. We can see the horse finished 3rd in its last race on the 10th January 2021 underlined in brown so LV=3 and passes this filter.

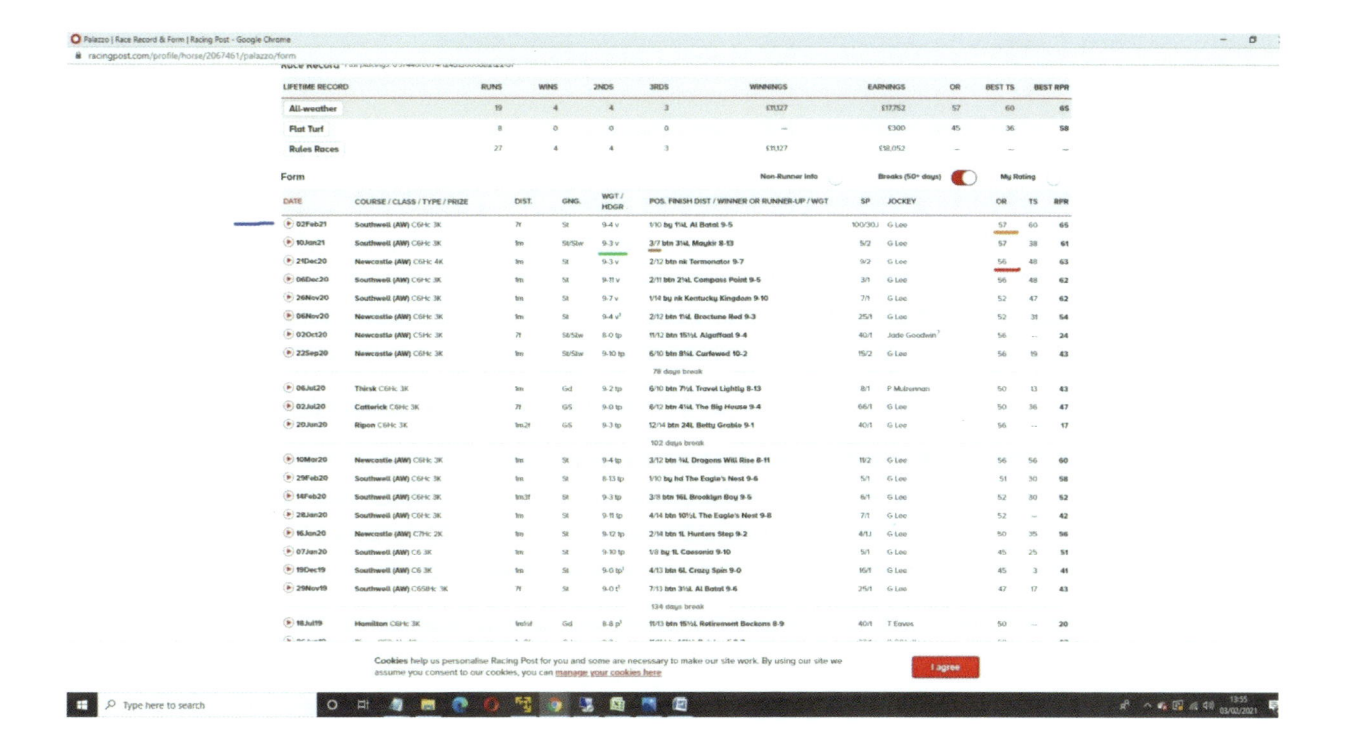

[screenshot of Racing Post race record & form page for the horse Palazzo]

So to summarize the horse Palazzo's four horse form variables are,

CV=7 WV=1 BV=1 LV=3

The value of each horse form variable is within the acceptable range. Please note all four variables must be in the acceptable range for the horse to qualify as a potential bet.

CV acceptable range <=7

WV acceptable range <=1

BV acceptable range >=0 and <=4

LV acceptable range <=5

Any horse that has a horse form variable not in the acceptable range you ignore the horse in the race.

Let us examine the other horses in the race Palazzo won on the 2nd February 2021.

Horse	Form Variables	Has Horse Qualified (Y/N)	
Al Batal	CV=12 WV=4 BV=3 LV=9	N	CV>7
Glory Of Paris	CV=22 WV=10 BV=-5 LV=4	N	CV>7
Mayson Mount	CV=12 WV=5 BV=1 LV=6	N	CV>7
Daafy	CV=12 WV=-2 BV=3 LV=1	N	CV>7

De Bruyne Horse CV=16 WV=-5 BV=-3 LV=3	N	CV>7
Dors Toyboy CV=10 WV=-3 BV=4 LV=2	N	CV>7
Shortbackandsides CV=25 WV=0 BV=1 LV=5	N	CV>7
Carriage Clock CV=26 WV=-10 BV=0 LV=8	N	CV>7
Amazon Princess CV=18 WV=6 BV=0 LV=11	N	CV>7

Note the above horses all failed on the CV variable value not within the acceptable range <=7

This was an easy race to assess not much work to do here.

I have outlined in detail an example race sometimes you will get 2 or 3 horses that meet the 4 horse form variable criteria when this situation arises I tend to back these on the Betfair exchange at larger decimal odds than what is available. I also combine this strategy with a back to lay to minimise my risk. As mentioned earlier you could dutch these horses for an equal profit it's up to you.

In the next chapter I will give example races without the screenshots as you should be familiar with the horse form reading guide. Please make sure you understand the Palazzo race above before reading the next chapter.

Some Example UK Handicap Horse Races

3rd February 2021 Warwick 4.40 Miss Heritage 7/2 Won

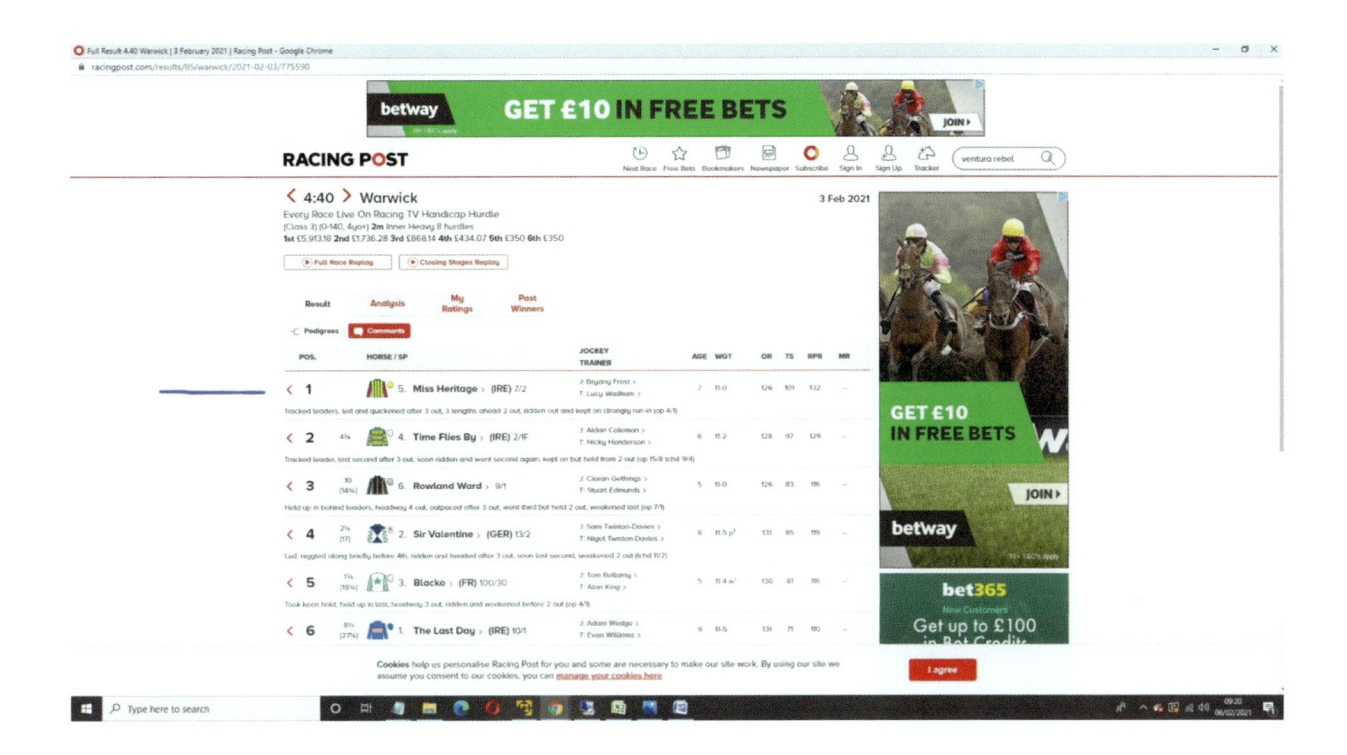

Horse	Form Variables	Has Horse Qualified (Y/N)	
Miss Heritage CV=6 WV=-5 BV=0 LV=2		Y	
Time Flies By CV=16 WV=9 BV=128 LV=9		N	CV > 7
Sir Valentine CV=8 WV=-3 BV=-2 LV=4		N	CV > 7
Blacko CV=11 WV=-6 BV=-3 LV=5		N	CV > 7
The Last Day CV=10 WV=1 BV=-11 LV=5		N	CV > 7
Roland Ward CV=18 WV=2 BV=-3 LV=2		N	CV > 7

This was an easy race to assess as apart from the winning horse Miss Heritage all horses failed on CV variable value being > 7. Analysing this race should have taken no more than 10 minutes and the horse won quite easily.

3rd February 2021 Kempton 5.55 Beauty Stone 14/1 Won

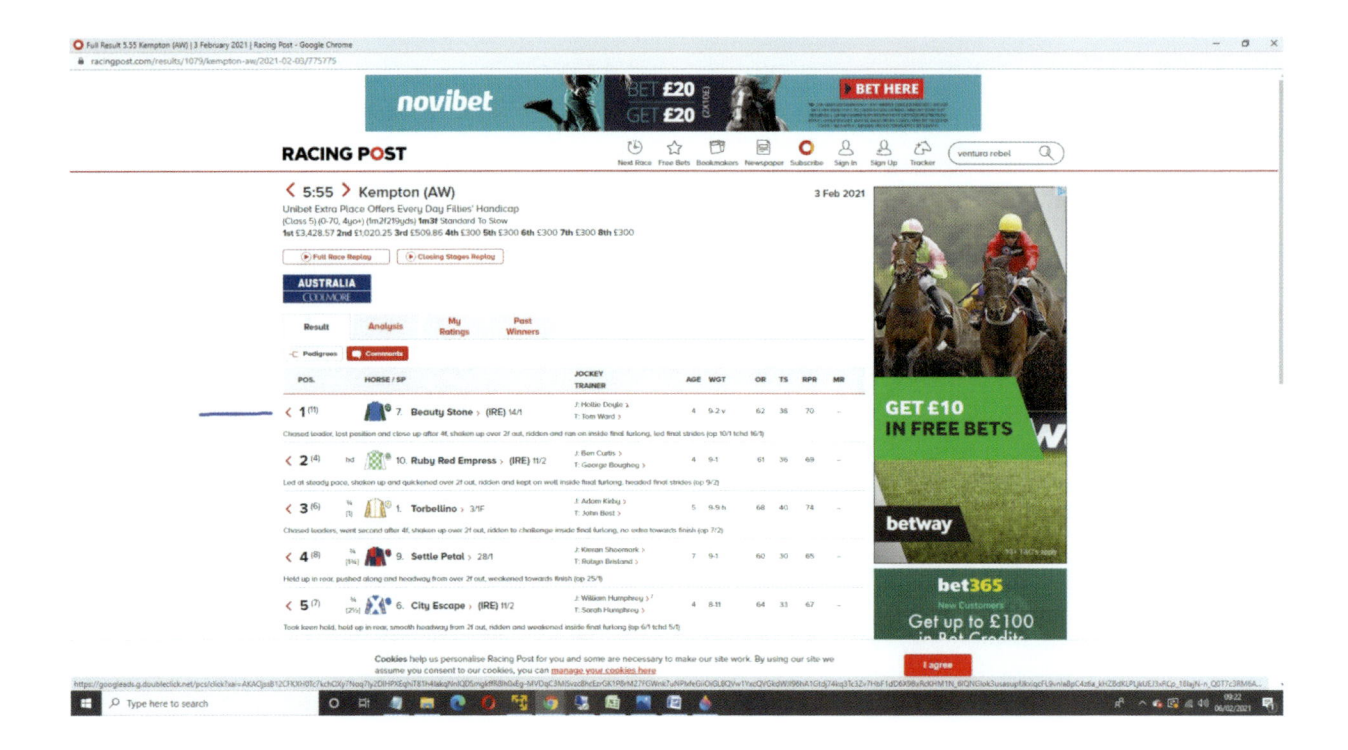

This was a great winner and even higher price on Betfair which I love to bet and trade.

This was another race that was easy to assess as all of the horses apart from the winner failed on the CV variable value.

Horse	Form Variables	Has Horse Qualified (Y/N)
Beauty Stone CV=7 WV=-3 BV=1 LV=4		Y
Torbellino CV=15 WV=-3 BV=1 LV=2		N
Angel Of Delight CV=15 WV=3 BV=-1 LV=-3		N
City Escape CV=9 WV=-3 BV=2 LV=3		N
Settle Petal CV=26 WV=-6 BV=0 LV=12		N
Iconic Belle CV=15 WV=2 BV=-5 LV=4		N
Filles De Fleur CV=17 WV=-7 BV=0 LV=4		N
Voi CV=10 WV=-1 BV=1 LV=5		N
Plansina CV=11 WV=-11 BV=0 LV=2		N
Ruby Red Empress CV=20 WV=-6 BV=0 LV=4		N

Good Reason CV=30 WV=5 BV=-8 LV=7   N

6th August 2020 Bath 4.40 Clem A 33/1 Won

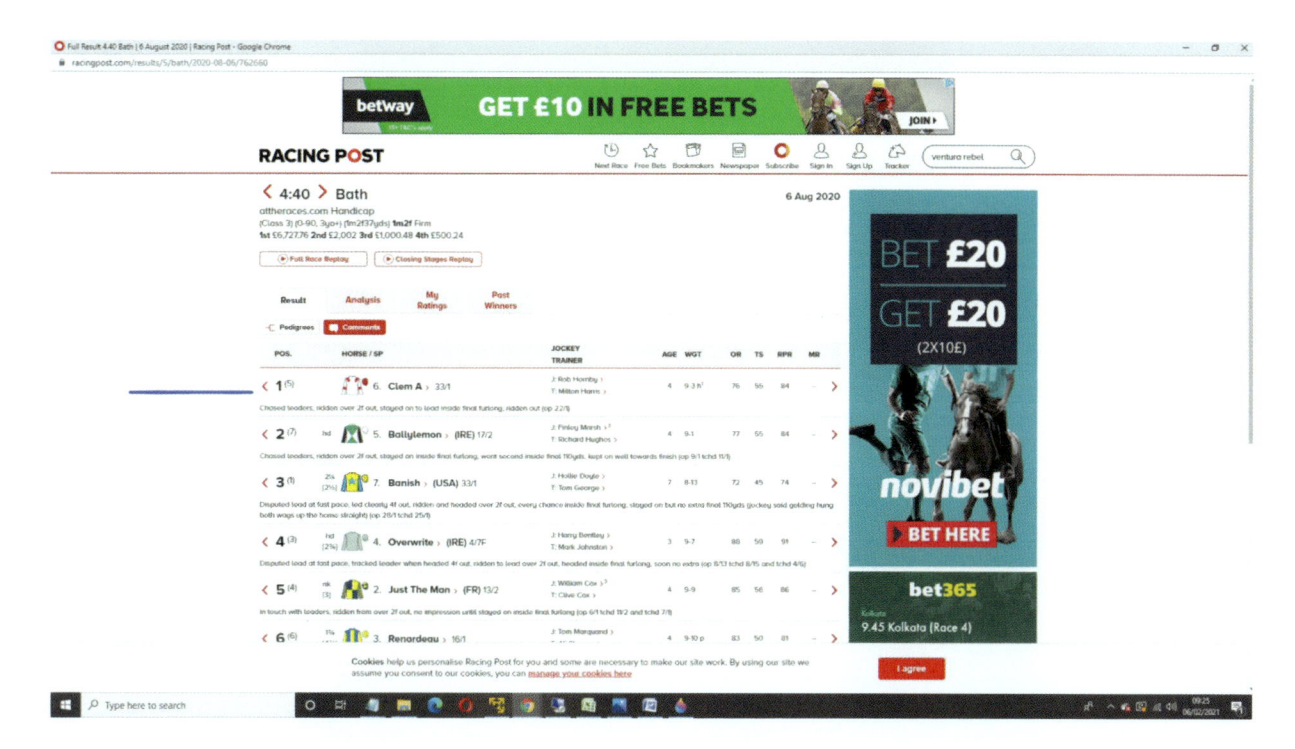

This was a horse I cleaned up on Betfair I could not believe the price on this horse that day.

Horse	Form Variables	Has Horse Qualified (Y/N)
Clem A CV=5 WV=-3 BV=4 LV=1		Y
Overwrite CV=11 WV=8 BV=-3 LV=2		N
Just The Man CV=19 WV=-2 BV=-5 LV=6		N
Ballylemon CV=27 WV-3 BV=-3 LV=9		N
Banish CV=24 WV=-7 BV=-5 LV=5		N
Dubai Instinct CV=25 WV=9 BV=2 LV=10		N
Renardeau CV=13 WV=-1 BV=-1 LV=10		N

27th January 2021 Lingfield 3.35 Outrage 6/4F Won

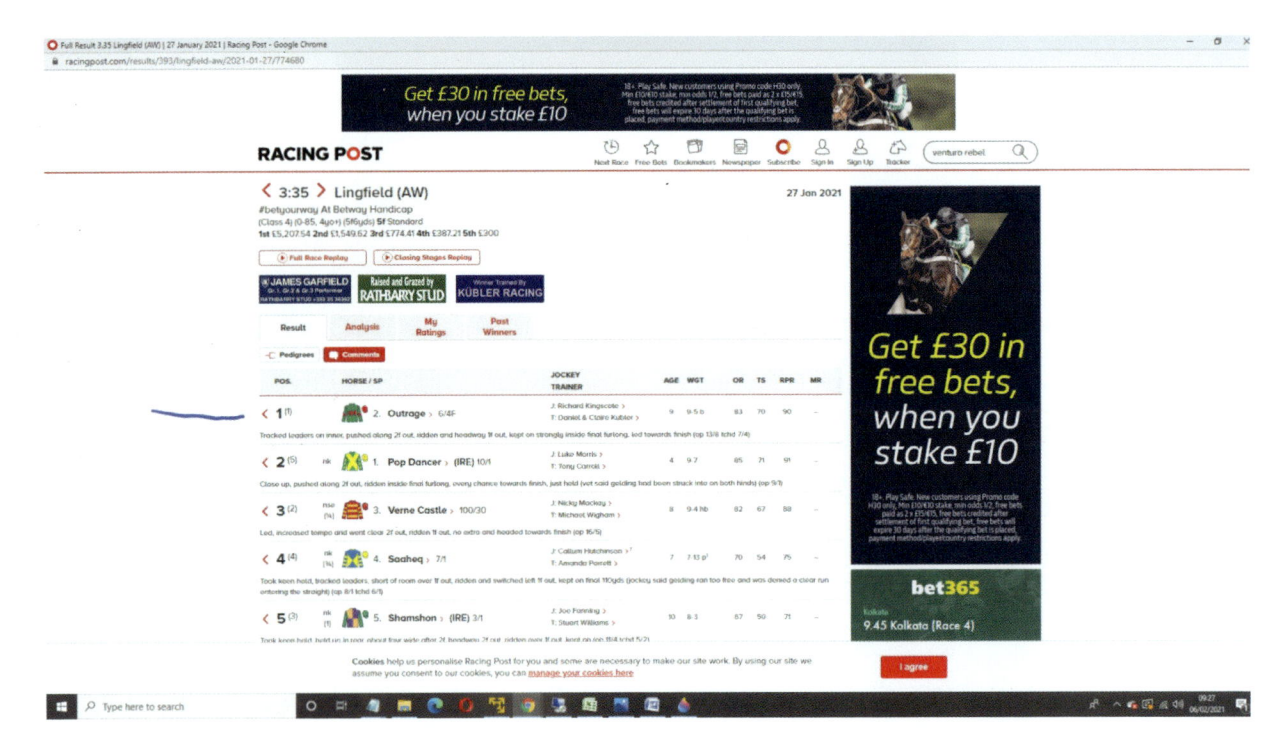

A short priced winner but it's a winner and always try and get a better price on Betfair pre-off or in-play.

Horse	Form Variables	Has Horse Qualified (Y/N)
Outrage	CV=6 WV=-2 BV=0 LV=2	Y
Pop Dancer	CV=19 WV=-2 BV=0 LV=12	N
Verne Castle	CV=10 WV=2 BV=2 LV=2	N
Saaheq	CV=13 WV=-13 BV=-3 LV=4	N
Shamshon	CV=8 WV=-15 BV=0 LV=2	N

25th January 2021 Kempton 6.45 Starshiba 11/2 Won

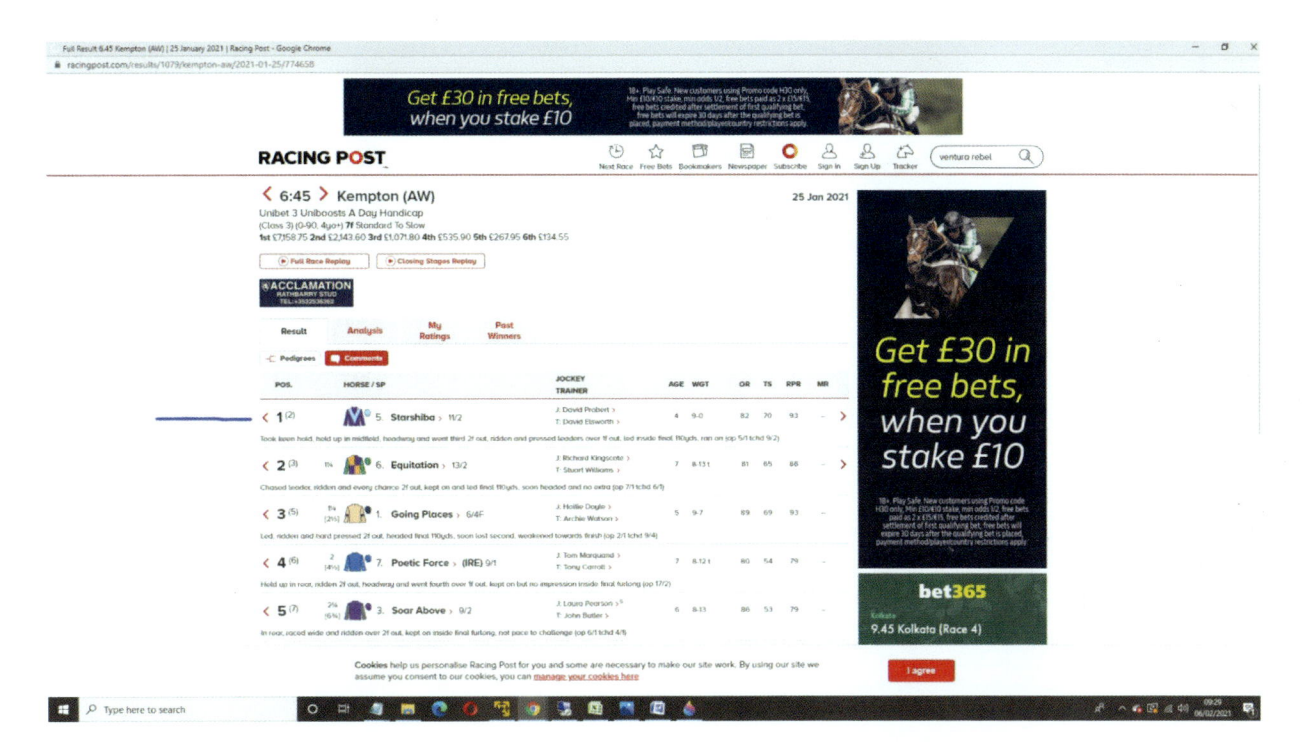

This is another race where most of the horses failed the CV variable value check.

Horse Form Variables	Has Horse Qualified (Y/N)
Starshiba CV=7 WV=-5 BV=0 LV=2	**Y**
Soar Above CV=9 WV=-2 BV=6 LV=3	N
Equitation CV=17 WV=-6 BV=-3 LV=6	N
Reaction Time CV=9 WV=-4 BV=14 LV=1	N
Going Places CV=7 WV=2 BV=89 LV=1	N
Poetic Force CV=16 WV=-7 BV=-1 LV=6	N
Golden Dragon CV=31 WV=1 BV=-9 LV=10	N
Thechildrenstrust CV=29 WV=-6 BV=-2 LV=11	N
Ice Age CV=17 WV=-17 BV=-4 LV=5	N

25th February 2021 Southwell 6.10 Gabrial The Devil 5/2 3rd

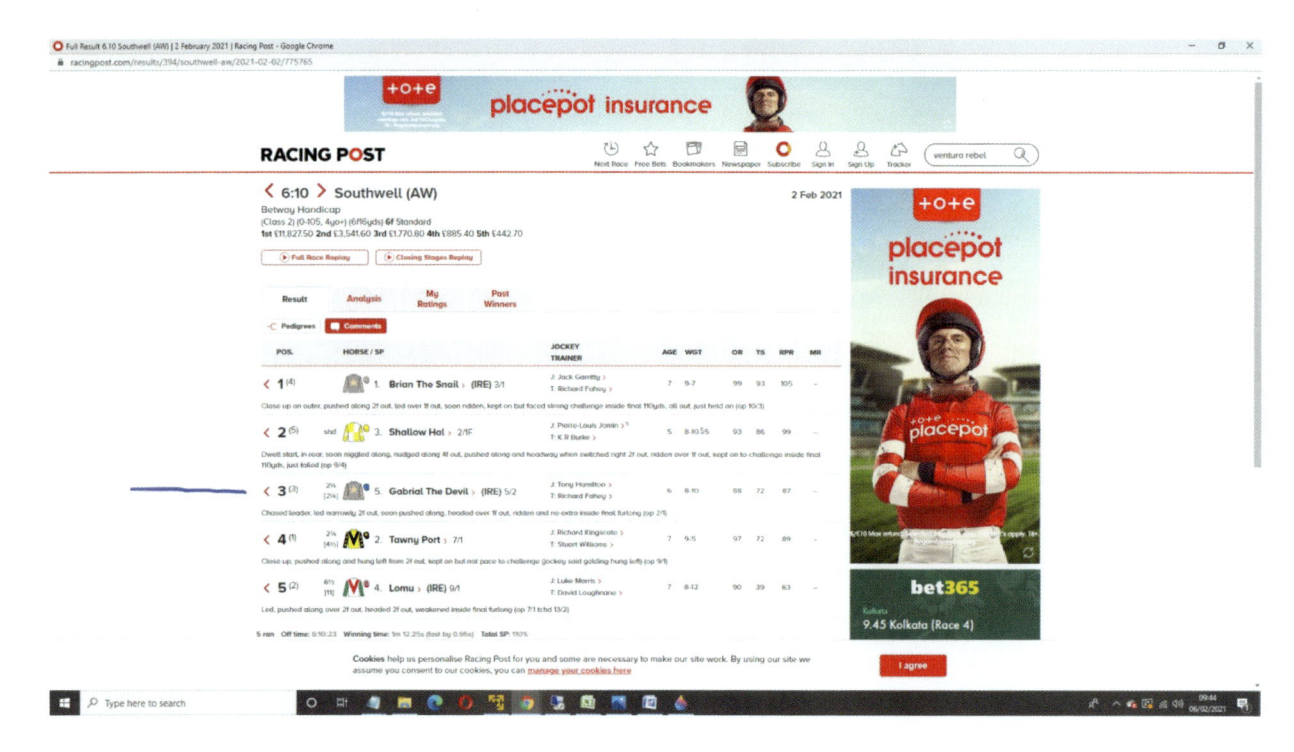

It is important to show losing bets not just winning bets in order to present this horse form guide honestly.

Horse	Form Variables	Has Horse Qualified (Y/N)
Gabrial The Devil CV=7 WV=-4 BV=3 LV=2		**Y**
Brian The Snail CV=8 WV=5 BV=1 LV=2		N
Tawny Port CV=11 WV=-4 BV=0 LV=3		N
Lomu CV=9 WV=-2 BV=1 LV=5		N
Shallow Hal CV=10 WV=-2 BV=4 LV=1		N

All horses failed on the CV variable apart from Gabrial The Devil what is interesting is that most of the horses passed on variables WV BV LV apart the horse Brian The Snail which failed on WV. This was a competitive race and I really should have left this race alone.

13th January 2021 Kempton 4.45 Nortonthorpe Boy 2/1F Won

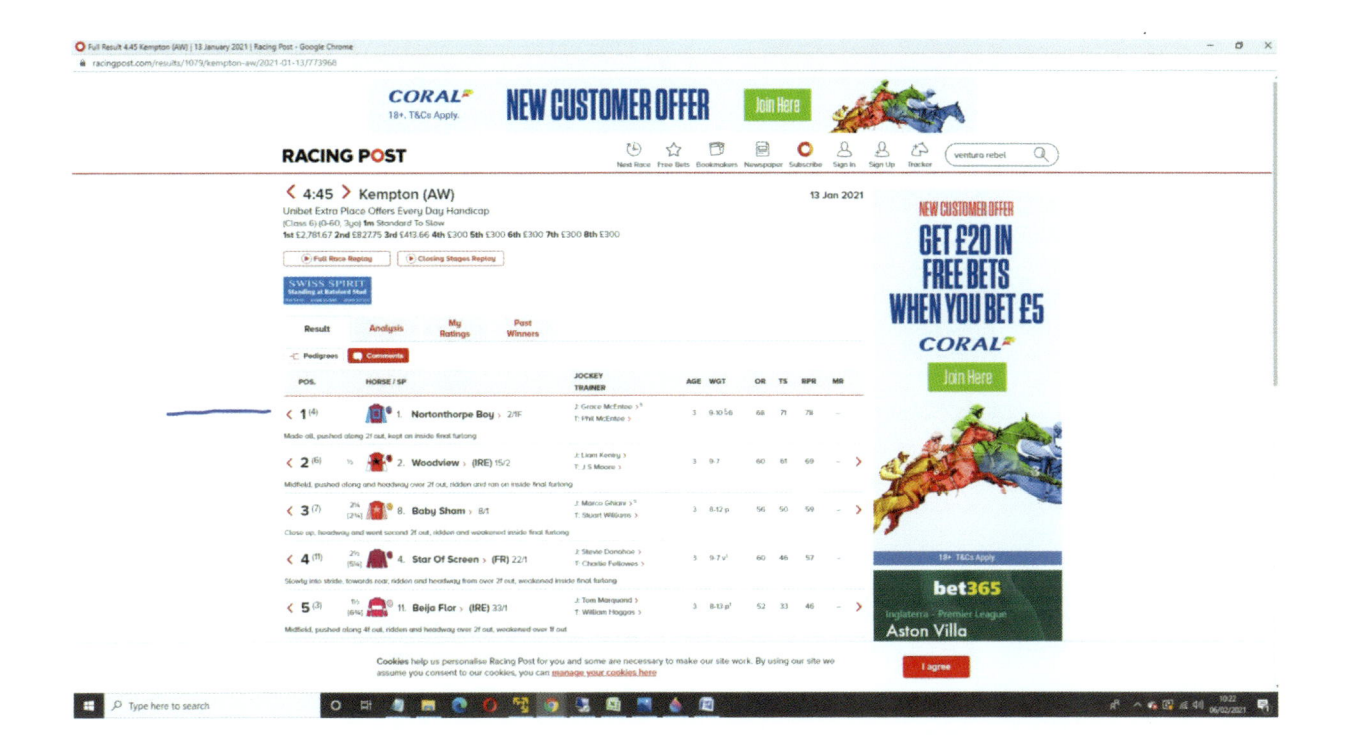

Horse	Form Variables	Has Horse Qualified (Y/N)
Nortonthorpe Boy CV=4 WV=-1 BV=4 LV=2		Y
Banoffee CV=14 WV=0 BV=0 LV=2		N
Hiroshi CV=11 WV=-4 BV=-1 LV=4		N
Zoolander CV=17 WV=4 BV=2 LV=8		N
Tamigi CV=15 WV=-1 BV=-1 LV=7		N
Woodview CV=14 WV=1 BV=60 LV=3		N
Baby Sham CV=17 WV=-10 BV=-3 LV=3		N
Real Dude CV=25 WV=-3 BV=54 LV=8		N
Star Of Screen CV=18 WV=9 BV=-5 LV=4		N
Hooves Like Jagger CV=24 WV=-3 BV=-11 LV=9		N
Beija Flor CV=18 WV=-1 BV=52 LV=4		N

Apart from the winner all the horses failed on the CV variable so another quick race to analyse.

15th January 2021 Newcastle 4.10 Loulin 8/1 Won

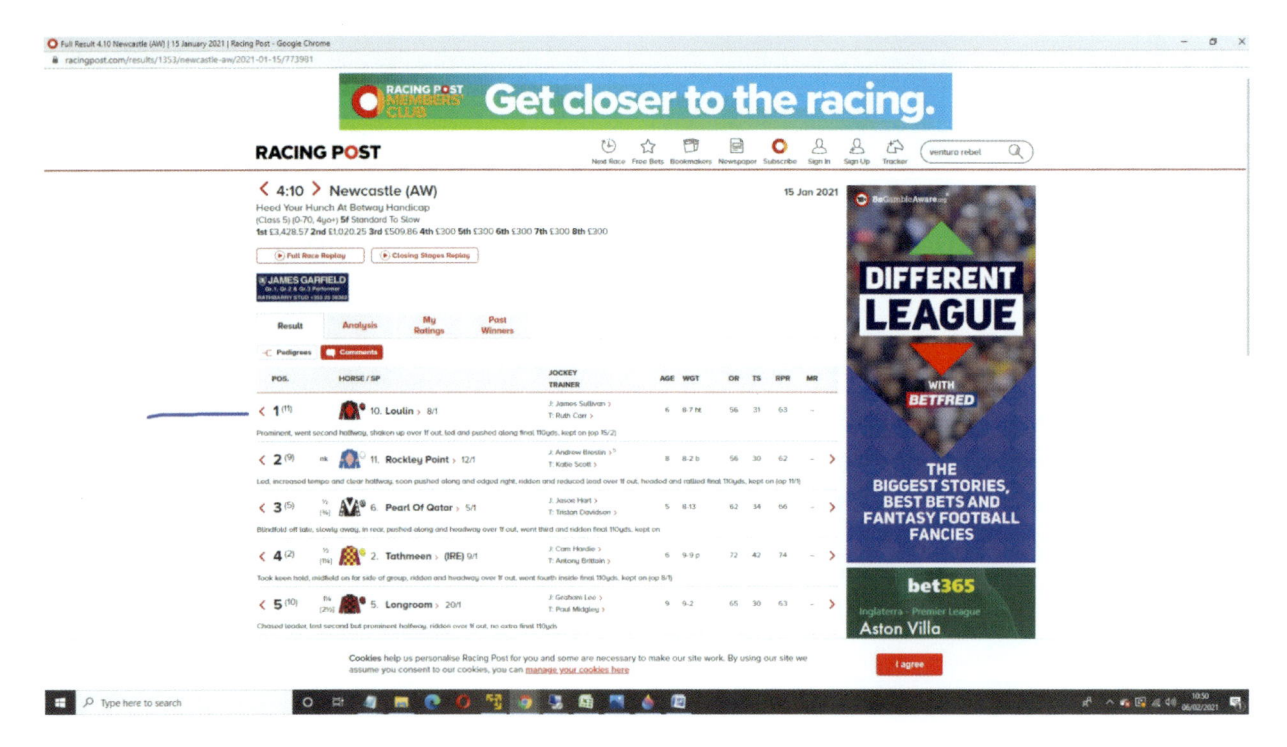

This was a great winner and a good price even bigger on the Betfair exchange.

Horse Form Variables	Has Horse Qualified (Y/N)
Loulin CV=6 WV=-1 BV=4 LV=1	Y
Tathmeen CV=13 WV=13 BV=-2 LV=6	N
Klopp CV=9 WV=-2 BV=2 LV=1	N
Kick On Kick On CV=13 WV=-1 BV=-1 LV=4	N
Primos Comet CV=16 WV=7 BV=-4 LV=4	N
Jan Van Hoof CV=33 WV=-7 BV=-4 LV=11	N
Longroom CV=11 WV=12 BV=-2 LV=5	N
Rockley Point CV=10 WV=-18 BV=3 LV=2	N
Pearl Of Qatar CV=12 WV=-4 BV=-1 LV=4	N
Global Humor CV=15 WV=-6 BV=-2 LV=4	N
Suwaan CV=26 WV=-7 BV=-6 LV=5	N
Charlemaine CV=33 WV=-2 BV=-10 LV=12	N

16th January 2021 Kempton 6.50 Lequinto 7/2 Won

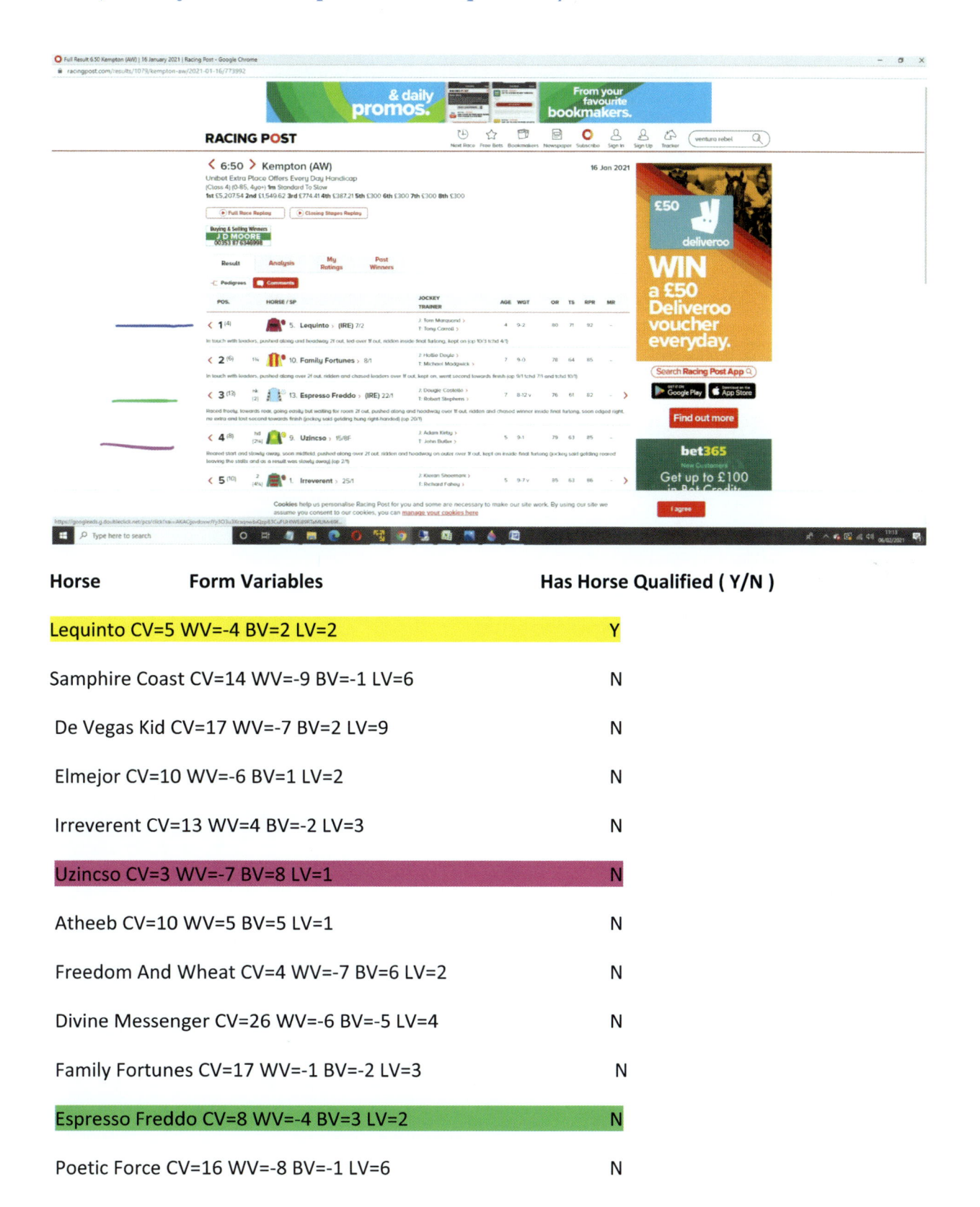

Horse	Has Horse Qualified (Y/N)
Lequinto CV=5 WV=-4 BV=2 LV=2	Y
Samphire Coast CV=14 WV=-9 BV=-1 LV=6	N
De Vegas Kid CV=17 WV=-7 BV=2 LV=9	N
Elmejor CV=10 WV=-6 BV=1 LV=2	N
Irreverent CV=13 WV=4 BV=-2 LV=3	N
Uzincso CV=3 WV=-7 BV=8 LV=1	N
Atheeb CV=10 WV=5 BV=5 LV=1	N
Freedom And Wheat CV=4 WV=-7 BV=6 LV=2	N
Divine Messenger CV=26 WV=-6 BV=-5 LV=4	N
Family Fortunes CV=17 WV=-1 BV=-2 LV=3	N
Espresso Freddo CV=8 WV=-4 BV=3 LV=2	N
Poetic Force CV=16 WV=-8 BV=-1 LV=6	N

The Met CV=14 WV=-7 BV=0 LV=3   N

Sherpa Trail CV=19 WV=-10 BV=-5 LV=8   N

This was a super race as it had a couple of angles that I have highlighted in different colours. The horse <mark style="background-color: yellow">Lequinto</mark> won the race but look at <mark style="background-color: lightgreen">Espresso Freddo</mark> placed 3rd at 22/1 this horse only failed on the CV variable which was 8 you can be flexible here with such tight margins on variable values. The favourite <mark style="background-color: magenta">Uzincso</mark> 15/8f finishing 4th.

16th January 2021 Lingfield 2.00 Black Medic 10/1 3rd

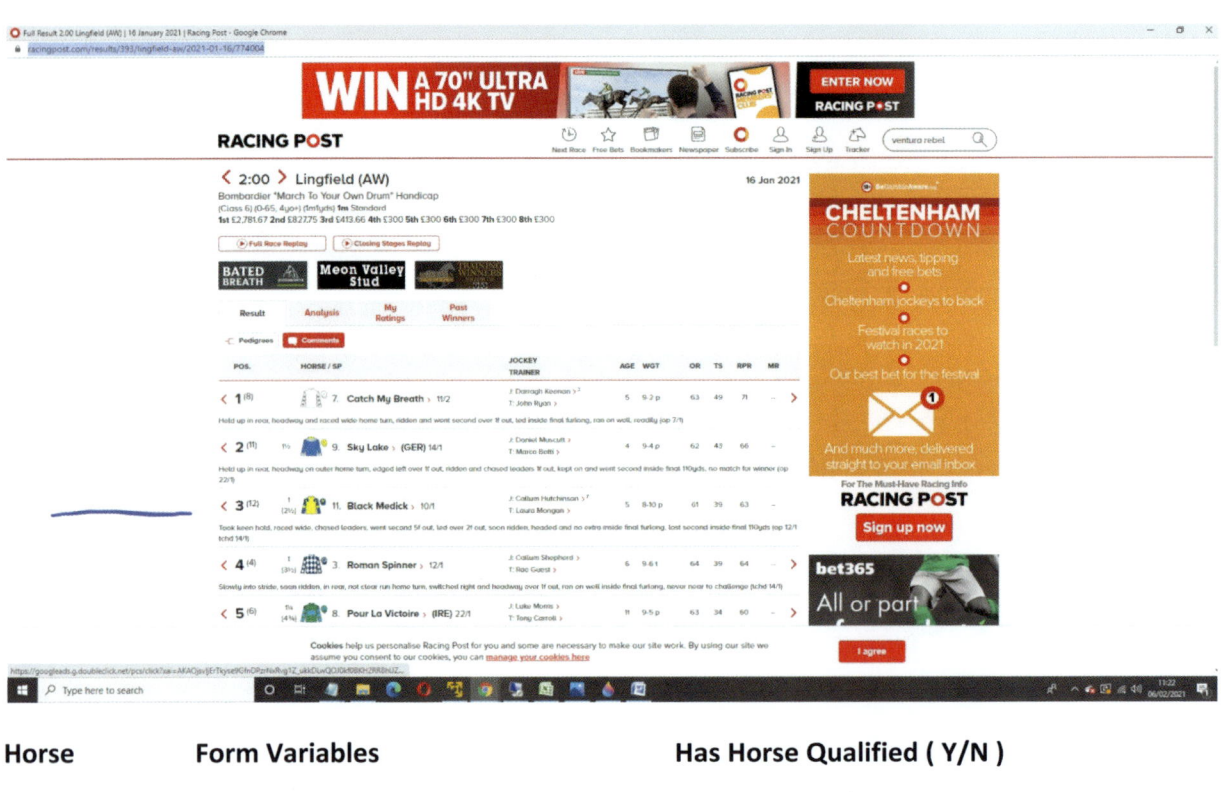

Horse	Form Variables	Has Horse Qualified (Y/N)
Black Medick CV=6 WV=-5 BV=2 LV=4		**Y**
Dutugamunu CV=14 WV=1 BV=3 LV=1		N
Pour La Victoire CV=12 WV=7 BV=-2 LV=5		N
Lunar Deity CV=11 WV=10 BV=4 LV=2		N
Winklemann CV=16 WV=-2 BV=3 LV=2		N
Debs Delight CV=15 WV=-2 BV=-2 LV=5		N
Quarry Beach CV=22 WV=10 BV=-5 LV=5		N

Roman Spinner CV=22 WV=8 BV=-5 LV=6   N

Catch My Breath CV=14 WV=1 BV=-2 LV=4   N

Sky Lake CV=17 WV=5 BV=-3 LV=3   N

Hibernian Warrior CV=26 WV=13 BV=-13 LV=6   N

Rhyme Scheme CV=16 WV=6 BV=-5 LV=5   N

6th February 2021 Sandown 3.30 Deise Aba 17/2 Won

A small horse race field but a great price on the winner.

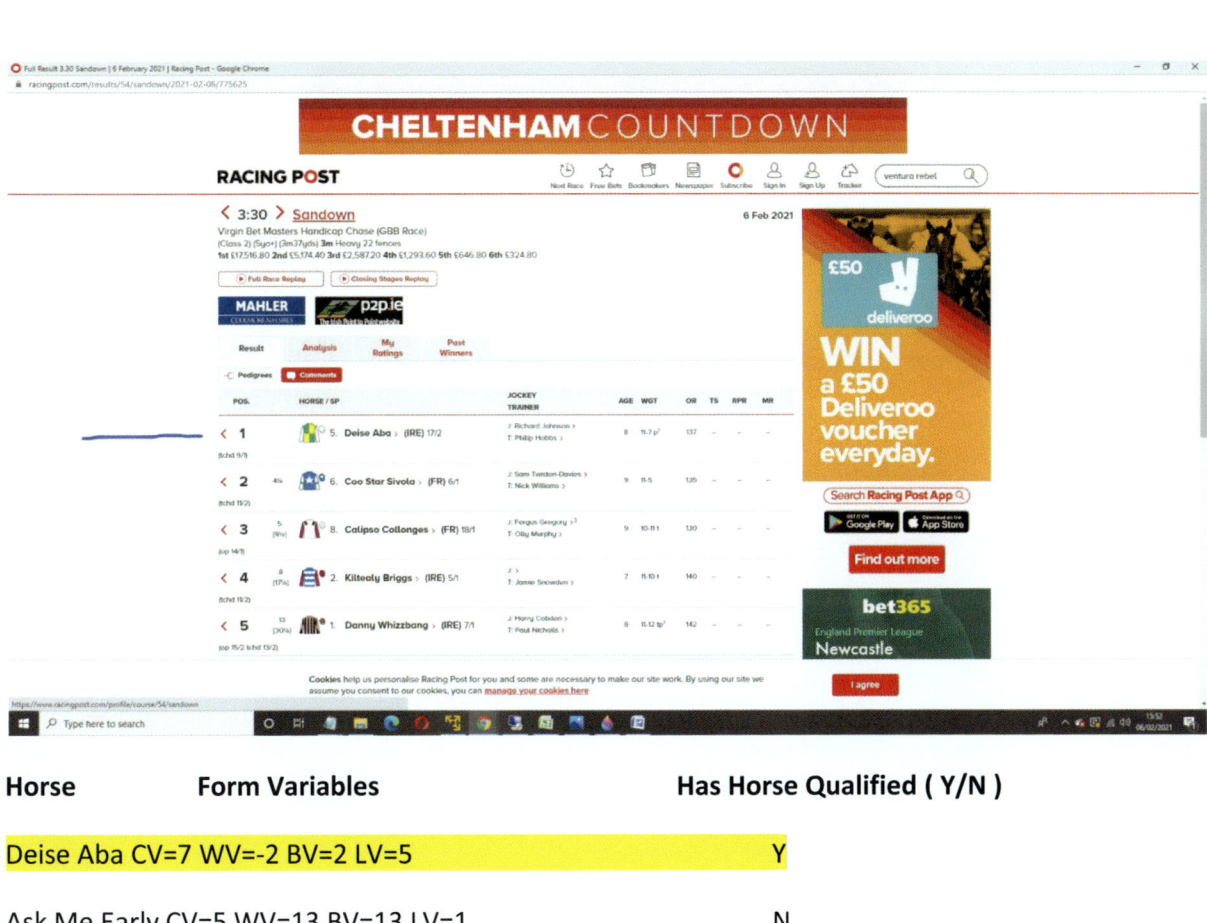

Horse	Form Variables	Has Horse Qualified (Y/N)
Deise Aba CV=7 WV=-2 BV=2 LV=5		Y
Ask Me Early CV=5 WV=13 BV=13 LV=1		N
Danny Whizzbang CV=13 WV=1 BV=-5 LV=7		N
Dominateur CV=23 WV=15 BV=-2 LV=13		N
A Toi Phil CV=9 WV=3 BV=-4 LV=4		N
Coo Star Sivola CV=17 WV=6 BV=-4 LV=5		N
Calipso Collonges CV=12 WV=14 BV=3 LV=4		N

6th February 2021 Lingfield 2.16 Symbolic Power 15/8F Won

Not a great price but still money in the bank.

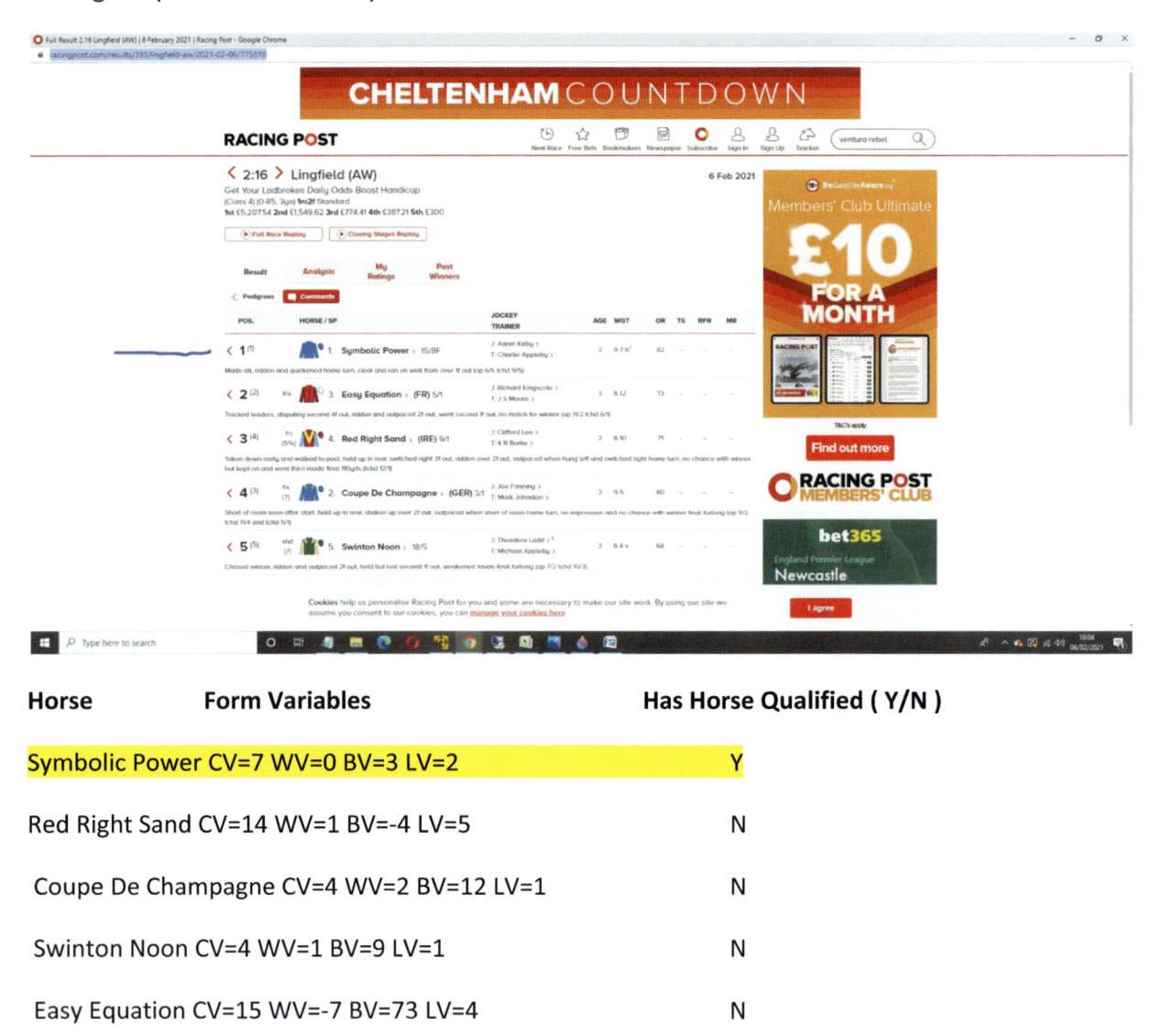

Horse	Form Variables	Has Horse Qualified (Y/N)
Symbolic Power CV=7 WV=0 BV=3 LV=2		Y
Red Right Sand CV=14 WV=1 BV=-4 LV=5		N
Coupe De Champagne CV=4 WV=2 BV=12 LV=1		N
Swinton Noon CV=4 WV=1 BV=9 LV=1		N
Easy Equation CV=15 WV=-7 BV=73 LV=4		N

21st September 2020 Wolverhampton 7.00 Aquascape 10/1 Won

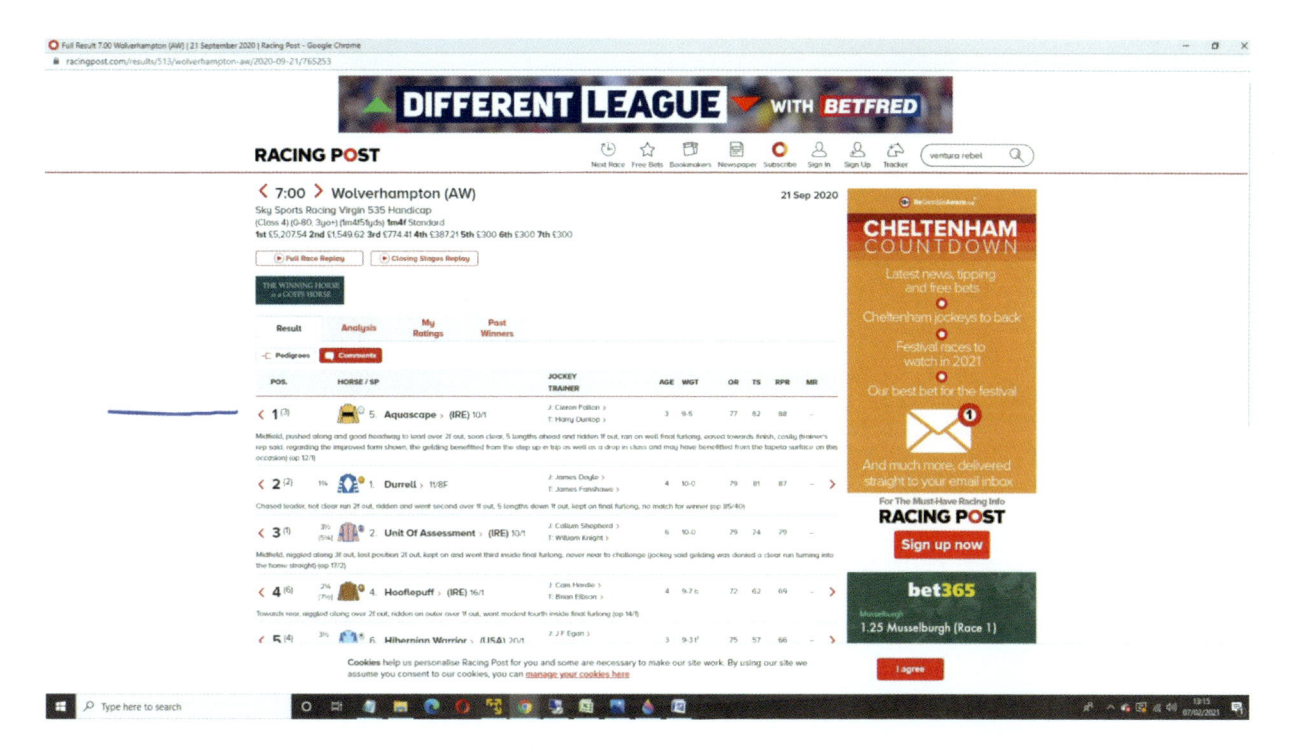

These are the winners that put a smile on your face considering the favourite 11/8F was at a short price don't follow the punting crowd!

Horse	Form Variables	Has Horse Qualified (Y/N)
Aquascape CV=7 WV=1 BV=3 LV=2		Y
Hooflepuff CV=21 WV=10 BV=-2 LV=10		N
Point In Time CV=16 WV=-1 BV=-1 LV=4		N
Unit Of Assessment CV=14 WV=8 BV=2 LV=3		N
Durrell CV=16 WV=2 BV=-4 LV=5		N
Hibernian Warrior CV=16 WV=2 BV=-3 LV=6		N
Kesarina CV=12 WV=-7 BV=2 LV=2		N

23rd September 2020 Goodwood 1.50 Hortzadar 3/1 Won

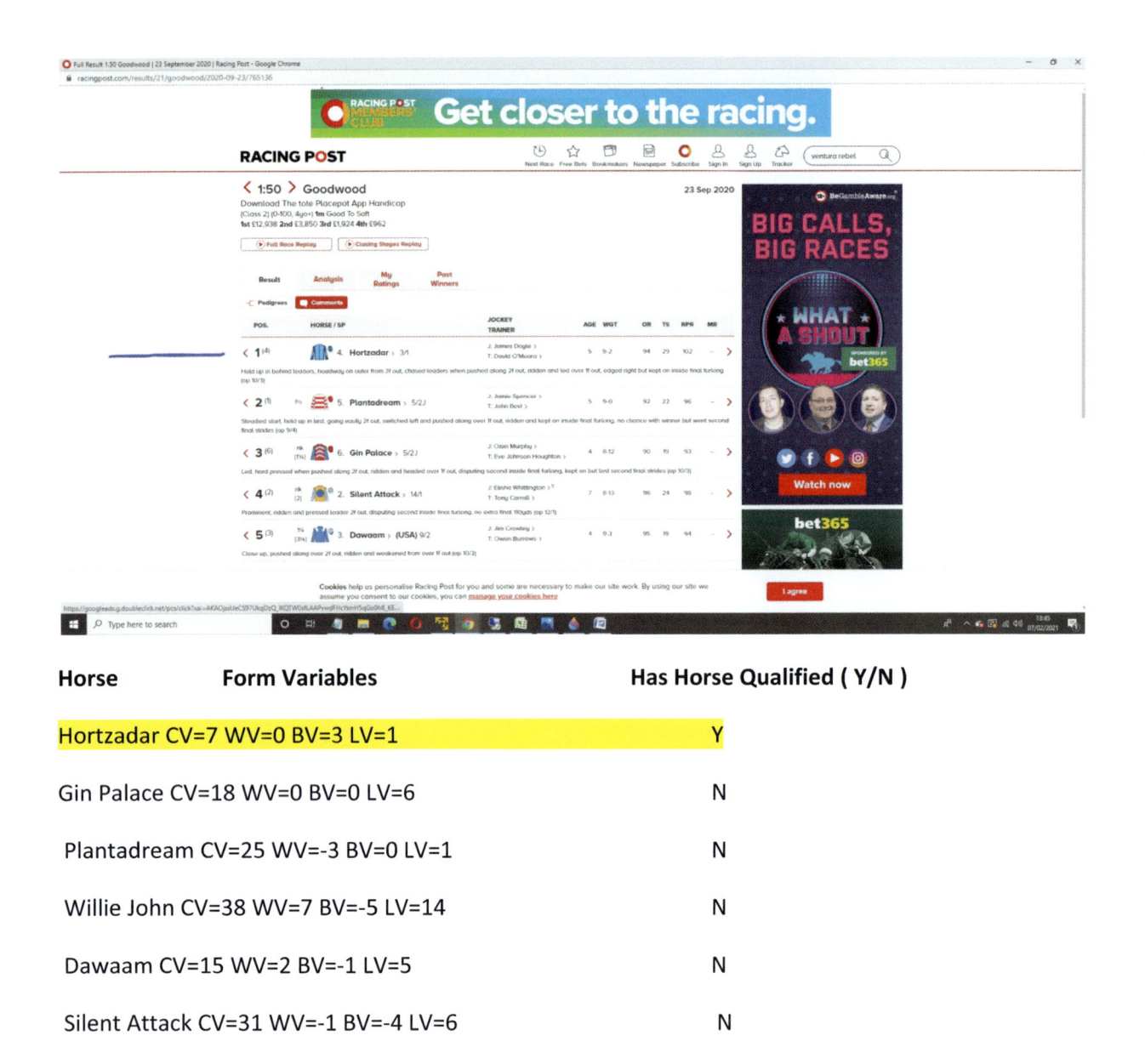

Horse	Form Variables	Has Horse Qualified (Y/N)
Hortzadar CV=7 WV=0 BV=3 LV=1		Y
Gin Palace CV=18 WV=0 BV=0 LV=6		N
Plantadream CV=25 WV=-3 BV=0 LV=1		N
Willie John CV=38 WV=7 BV=-5 LV=14		N
Dawaam CV=15 WV=2 BV=-1 LV=5		N
Silent Attack CV=31 WV=-1 BV=-4 LV=6		N

25th September 2020 Haydock 2.15 Vulcan 2/1F Won

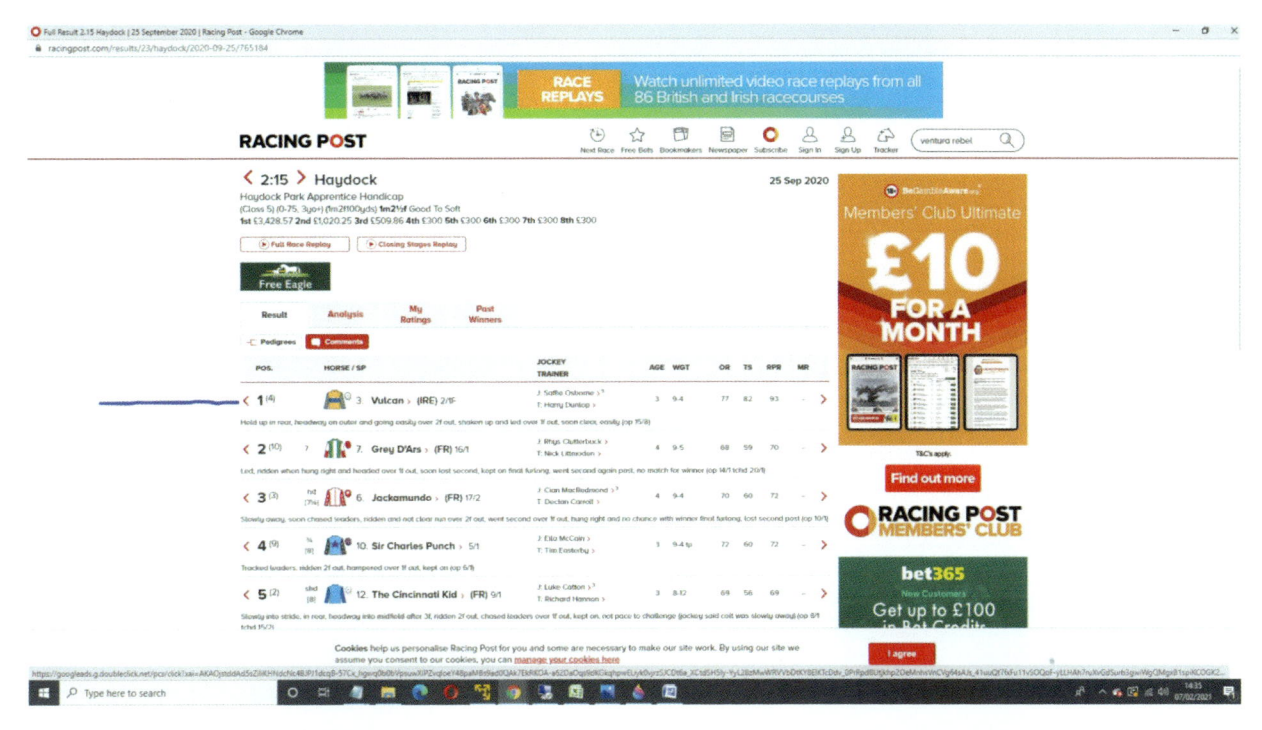

Horse	Has Horse Qualified (Y/N)
Vulcan CV=5 WV=1 BV=4 LV=1	Y
Gamesters Icon CV=12 WV=11 BV=-2 LV=6	N
Jackamundo CV=25 WV=3 BV=-4 LV=9	N
The Cincinnati Kid CV=16 WV=-1 BV=69 LV=7	N
Central City CV=18 WV=0 BV=-2 LV=3	N
Straitouttacompton CV=3 WV=5 BV=8 LV=1	N
Sir Charles Punch CV=13 WV=3 BV=-1 LV=4	N
Bombero CV=25 WV=-6 BV=-4 LV=8	N
Mahanakhon Power CV=21 WV=-5 BV=72 LV=6	N
Grey DArs CV=17 WV=-6 BV=-2 LV=3	N
Silent Performance CV=14 WV=8 BV=76 LV=4	N
Guildhall CV=22 WV=2 BV=-3 LV=10	N

Using The Horse Form Guide In UK Non Handicap Horse Races

I mentioned earlier that we use this horse form guide in UK Handicap horse races but you can also use this very effective horse form guide in UK non handicap horse races like novice and graded races. I personally like handicap horse races since I started betting in my 20's. You use the horse form guide in exactly the same way for UK handicap and UK non handicap races and it does find some large priced winners.

An example of a UK non handicap horse race below.

7th February 2021 Musselburgh 3.25 Bareback Jack 5/2 Won

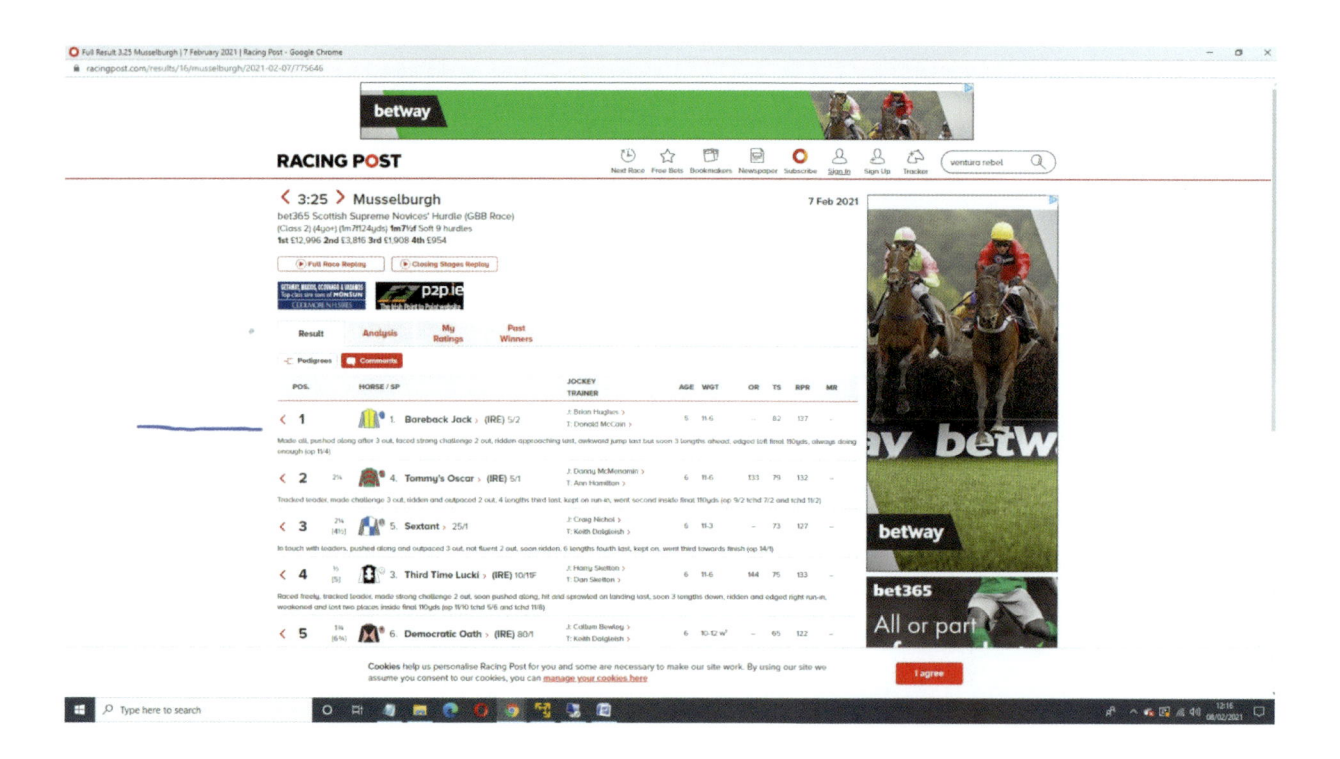

Horse	Form Variables	Has Horse Qualified (Y/N)
Bareback Jack CV=2 WV=-2 BV=1 LV=1		Y
Third Time Lucki CV=4 WV=-2 BV=15 LV=1		N
Tommys Oscar CV=3 WV=3 BV=133 LV=1		N
Belfast Banter CV=8 WV=13 BV=8 LV=5		N
Sextant CV=1 WV=5 - LV=1		N
Democratic Oath CV=9 WV=-2 - LV=3		N

Using The Horse Form Guide Additional Filters

Using the horse form guide will find plenty of winners but a word of caution when you have qualified a selection for a race it's optional to perform extra checks on horse form it's up to you. I will give you an example of this I would ignore a horse if it had not run for a year. You could check if the horse had won over the distance it's entirely up to you which might add clout in confirming this selection.

The horse form variable CV states a horse must have a value of 7 or less but please do not always discount horses with CV value of 8 or 9 as these find great winners as well. In a nutshell try to be flexible when reading horse form.

I always use the Betfair betting exchange to get the better prices pre-off and in-play this is something I always stress in all of my books.

Final note enjoy the book and you will find winners.

Recommended Sites

https://www.betbotpro.com/

https://www.betextrader.com/

COPYRIGHT 2021 MCHJAP LTD All Rights Reserved.
COPYRIGHT of this publication is strictly reserved.
No part of this publication may be reproduced or transmitted.

Printed in Great Britain
by Amazon